ROBIN'S STORY

Physical Abuse and Seeing the Doctor

by Deborah Anderson
and Martha Finne

Illustrated by Jeanette Swofford

Dillon Press, Inc.   Minneapolis, Minnesota 55415

To Robert tenBensel, M.D., for his long years of dedication and work in the field of child abuse and neglect

Illustrations courtesy of Hennepin County Medical Society Auxiliary, Inc.

Library of Congress Cataloging in Publication Data

Anderson, Deborah, 1946-
  Robin's story.

  Summary: Describes a girl who is physically abused by her mother and what happens when she sees a doctor. Includes an adult resource guide and sources of help for children.
  1. Child abuse—Juvenile literature.   2. Child abuse—Prevention—Juvenile literature.   3. Abused children—Medical examinations—Juvenile literature. [1. Child abuse]
  I. Finne, Martha. II. Title.
  HV713.A53   1986   362.7'044   85-25383
  ISBN 0-87518-321-2

Dillon Press, Inc., 242 Portland Avenue South
Minneapolis, Minnesota 55415

Printed in the United States of America
  2 3 4 5 6 7 8 9 10 95 94 93 92 91 90 89 88 87

Contents

Robin's Story

Last year, Mom was always getting
angry at me. When she did, she would
hit me and yell at me. Mom said she
worked hard and always felt tired. When
she was tired, she yelled and hit the
most. Sometimes her hand left red
marks, and once in a while she used a
belt. She called them spankings. I
thought they were really beatings.

One night I was playing with my friend
Tana and came home after dark.

When I came in, Mom started yelling right away. She was really mad. "Don't you ever listen?" she yelled. "You *know* you have to be home for dinner. You know the rules. Where did you go? Didn't you think I'd be worried about you?" She was walking back and forth in the kitchen.

"But, Mom," I said, "it was Tana's fault, too. She said we should go—"

Mom said, "Tana doesn't live here. You do!"

I said, "But, Mom—"

"Don't argue with me!" Mom yelled. Then, she threw our cookie tin at me. I ducked, but the tin hit my head. It

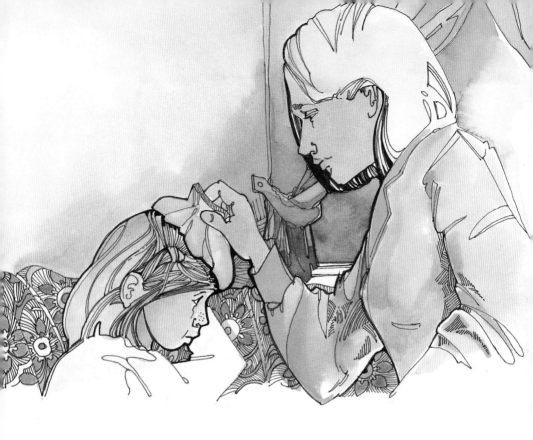

REALLY hurt. Cookies were all over the floor. And I was scared, because there was blood on my forehead. I started crying.

Mom ran across the kitchen to me. "I'm sorry, I'm sorry," she said. "I didn't mean to hit you." She put some ice in a cloth and put the cloth on my head.

After a while, the cut didn't bleed any more. My head hurt, though.

Later, it was time for bed. Mom came in and sat on my bed. "Does your head hurt now?" she asked.

"No," I said, even though it still did hurt a little. Lots of times I didn't tell her things. Sometimes she got angry again and would yell or spank.

"Robin, you know I didn't mean to hurt you," Mom said.

"I know," I told her. But I didn't think she was sorry. She always forgot by the next time she got angry.

"If anyone asks what happened tomorrow at school, tell them you ran into a door," Mom said. "Okay?"

"Okay," I said. "Good night."

"I mean it," Mom said. "Other people might make trouble."

"Okay, Mom, I'll tell them about the door," I said.

"That's my girl." Mom smiled then and kissed me goodnight.

The next day at school, I was one of the first kids there. Ms. Andrews, my teacher, looked at me and asked me to come up to her desk. She said in a quiet voice, "Your forehead looks as if it hurts. Can you tell me what happened?"

"I forget," I said. Then I remembered what Mom said. "Oh, I remember. I ran into a door," I told her.

"That cut looks serious to me," she said. "How did you run into a door? Weren't you looking?"

"I guess not," I said. I didn't like to tell lies. I looked at the floor and hoped Ms. Andrews would let me sit down. The other kids were coming in.

"Robin," she said, "that cut needs a bandage on it. I'm going to send you to Ms. French, our social worker, so she can look at it. She might ask your mother to take you to the clinic." Then she gave me a pass to the office.

I had never talked to Ms. French before. We all knew her. Kids who had talked with her said they liked her.

When I got to the office, I had to wait. I was scared Ms. French would ask me questions about the cut. Would Ms. French believe me? What if she knows I'm lying? I wondered.

"Well, now, Robin," Ms. French said when I came in, "let's look at that cut." She touched my head. "I think it needs to have a bandage on it. It looks painful. Does it hurt?"

"Not anymore," I said. That was the truth, at least.

"Can you tell me what happened?" she asked.

"I ran into the door," I said. "I didn't watch where I was going."

"Oh," she said. She was quiet for a minute. I wondered if she believed me.

Then Ms. French said, "Robin, my job is to help kids. Sometimes kids get sent here when they're in trouble in class. Sometimes they forget their homework a lot, or lose their books, or are late or absent too much. Often, after we talk, I find out that the kid is getting into trouble at school because of problems at home. I try to help kids who have those problems. Do you understand what I'm talking about?"

"Yes," I said.

Ms. French asked me if my mom and dad worked. I told her that Mom worked in a store, but Dad didn't live with us. She asked who watched me after school, and I told her I watched myself until Mom got home. Then she wanted to know if there were rules set up about after school. Could I go out? Did I have to tell Mom where I was going? I told her I could go out, but that I had to be back for supper.

"What did you do after school yesterday?" asked Ms. French.

"I went to Tana's house," I said.

"Did your mom know where you were?" asked Ms. French. I said no.

"What happens when you don't follow the rules?" said Ms. French.

I didn't want to tell. "Mom gets mad," I finally said to her.

"What happens when your mom gets mad?" Ms. French wanted to know.

I was quiet then. She doesn't believe me about the door. What should I say? I wondered. I don't want to get Mom into trouble.

"Sometimes she yells," I told her. "Sometimes she spanks me."

"Robin," Ms. French said, "if something else happened, could you tell me about it?" I shook my head no. "Did something else happen last night?" Yes, I nodded. I couldn't talk. I couldn't look at her, either.

"What did happen?" she asked.

"Mom threw a cookie tin and hit me," I said. Then I felt awful. I had told! "But Mom didn't mean to."

Then she asked, "How do you know that?"

"It was my fault. I made her angry because I went to a friend's house and came home really late. Mom said she was sorry afterwards, and she put some ice on the cut. She was mad because I stayed out too late with my friend," I told her.

Ms. French just listened. Then she said, "Robin, I want to explain some things to you. Adults are not supposed to hurt children, no matter how angry they get, and no matter what the child has done. Sometimes an adult does hurt a child. If it's not an accident, it's called child abuse. There are laws to protect children from child abuse."

"Is the cut on my head child abuse?" I asked. I thought, What if she thinks Mom is a bad mom?

"It is abusive to throw a cookie tin at you, but that doesn't mean your mom is a bad person or a bad mother. It does mean that we must see that this doesn't happen again. Your mom can get help to stop throwing things at you. I'm going to call your mom now. You should see the doctor in case you need stitches."

Ms. French had me wait for Mom in the play area near her office. I was afraid Mom would be mad at me when she came. She had told me to say the cut was from running into a door. I didn't mean to tell what Mom did, but Ms. French kept asking questions.

Pretty soon Mom came. She looked worried. Ms. French asked us both to come into the office. Then Ms. French told my mom she knew how I got the cut on my head. I didn't look at Mom. Ms. French said she would help my mom.

Mom looked at me and said, "I asked
her not to tell." She sounded a little
angry. "I really didn't mean to hurt her.
I've been under a lot of stress. This
won't happen again."

Ms. French said, "I have to report this to Child Protection Services. There's a law that says I must. But first, Robin needs to see a doctor for that cut. Do you have a family doctor?" Mom shook her head no. "Then I'd like you to see Dr. Barton at the St. John's Clinic. I'll call and tell her you're on the way," said Ms. French.

On the way to the doctor, Mom was quiet. So was I. When we got to the clinic there were lots of people. I wondered if they knew what happened to me.

"How does your head feel?" Mom asked.

"It hurts a little," I said. Then I asked, "Do you think I'll have to get stitches? Will it hurt?"

"I don't know," Mom answered. "We'll both go together and talk to the doctor. I'll stay right there if you have to get stitches."

Then the nurse called us. She led us to

where the doctor was sitting.

Dr. Barton was a woman. She was nice to Mom and me. Dr. Barton asked how I got the cut, and Mom told the truth this time. I was glad about that.

To examine me, the doctor felt all over my head. She used something like a little flashlight and looked into my eyes. Then she said she wanted to check me over some more. After she looked me over front and back, she said I could get dressed.

"Now you'll need a few stitches on that cut, Robin. We can do that right here, and the nurse will help. This only takes a few minutes. We'll put something on the cut so it won't hurt too much."

Mom held my hand while the stitches were put in. It wasn't too bad, but it did hurt.

Then Dr. Barton said, "Mrs. Stevens, I'd like you to wait outside while I talk to Robin for a few minutes. Is that okay with you, Robin?"

"Yes," I said. But I wondered what she wanted. I was still scared Mom was going to be in trouble.

"Robin, getting a cut on your head is pretty serious when it's from something your mother did," Dr. Barton said. "Has anything like that happened before?"

"No," I said. "Mom never threw anything at me before."

"What happens when your mom gets mad?" she asked.

"Sometimes I get spanked. She uses a belt sometimes, when I do things I'm not supposed to do."

"Your mom used a belt? Have you ever had bruises?" Dr. Barton asked.

"I forget," I said. "Mostly, Mom just yells a lot. When she hits me, she says she's sorry afterwards."

"Robin, I have to report about your cut to a Child Protection social worker downtown. They can give your mom some help. They'll help you, too, so that you don't get hurt anymore. When she disciplines you, your mom needs to stop hitting. I see things like this happen to kids quite often. The law says I have to report it."

"Will they take me away from my mom?" I asked. I remembered one boy who had to go to a foster home. I felt scared that that might happen to me.

"No, I don't think so," said Dr. Barton. "Your mom seems to really care about you. She probably wants to learn not to get so angry."

"I don't want to leave my mom," I said. "I don't want anybody to think my mom's a bad mom."

Then I asked, "Do you really see other kids who have been hurt by their parents?" It made me feel better that I wasn't the only one.

"Yes, Robin, I do," she said. "It happens to a lot of kids, even babies. When we report it and the parents get help, things do change. The kids don't get hurt anymore."

"How do you know a baby was hurt by the mom or dad? Babies can't talk," I said.

She said, "Some bruises or even cuts are from accidents. But if a doctor knows about physical abuse, he or she knows what to look for. Some parents tell me about hurting their children. Other parents won't tell the truth. It is much harder to help parents who lie.

"Your mom said she threw the cookie tin at you. To say she did it is the first step for help. She even said she was sorry, and that is a second step. Now it is easier for her to get the help and learn not to hit when she is angry.

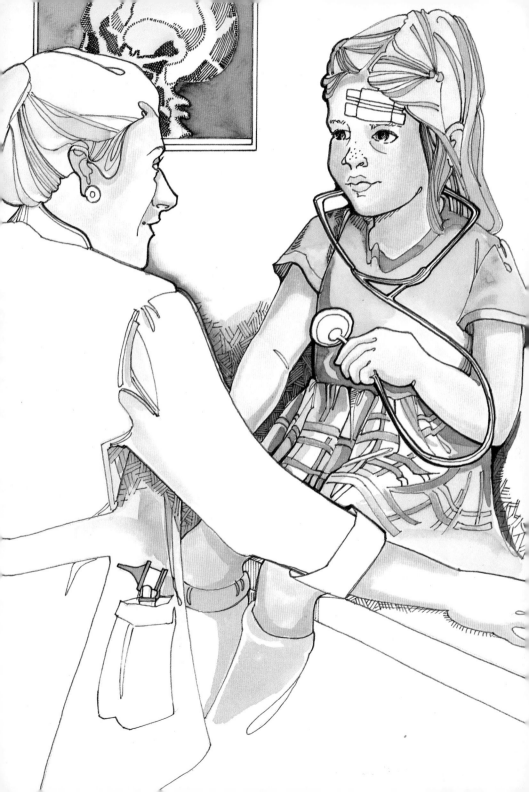

"All parents need to say no to children at times. But, hitting and hurting doesn't make children behave well," said Dr. Barton.

Then she asked, "Were you afraid when you came here today, Robin?"

I said, "Yes. I thought I'd get Mom into trouble. I don't want to be taken away from my mom."

"Don't you worry about that. Now a person from the Child Protection Services will come to see your mother. He or she will talk to you, too. This is the hard part right now—to tell so many people what happened to you. But telling will help make it better with you and your mom. I'm going to see you again in five days to check on your cut and see how things are going. Now, you can go out to your mom. I'll see you next week." I went out and sat down. Then I waited while Mom talked to the doctor alone. When we left, Dr. Barton smiled at me.

The next day at school, I had to see Ms. French before going back to my classroom. She looked happy to see me. She wanted to see my head and talk about seeing the doctor.

"Dr. Barton was nice," I said. "I was afraid she would think my mom was bad. But she didn't. I like that doctor."

"Yes, Dr. Barton really does care about kids," said Ms. French. "We both do. I talked to the Child Protection worker who saw your mom. Did you like her when you met her?" I nodded yes.

"I think the problem with hitting will get better now, with a little time. I'm glad you told me the truth yesterday. Now you know you are not to blame. I know it was hard for you to tell." Then she hugged me. "I care about you, Robin. Now run along so you're not late. We'll talk again soon."

That was what happened when I was in second grade. It really was hard to tell about it, but I'm glad I told the truth.

Things at home did get better. Mom still gets angry sometimes. But, she doesn't blame me or hit me anymore. Now she says, "I'm angry, Robin, but it's not your fault." And she never hits me.

I love my mom a lot!

Children and Physical Abuse

In the story, Robin's mother hurt her, and it wasn't an accident. That happens to lots of children. Adults discipline children in many ways. Some ways are okay, but some are not. The ways that are not okay are called physical abuse. Here are some things for you to know about physical abuse.

- When children get marks on their bodies that are not from an accident, it is physical abuse. Here are some ways that might happen.

   Being hit with a belt, a stick, a cord, or a hand.

Being pushed or pulled hard.

Getting a cut like Robin's.

The marks might be a bruise, a cut, a welt, or a burn.

- Children do need to learn right from wrong. Parents and other adults, such as teachers, teach them to behave. When children do not behave, they might be disciplined. Some kinds of discipline are okay if the child is not hurt. That might be things like sitting on a chair, having a time out, being sent to a room, or not being able to watch TV.

But physical abuse of children is against the law in the United States. Adults do not have the right to hurt children. If you are getting hurt by an adult who takes care of you, it is important to tell someone about it. It is important to tell so that the hurting will stop.

- Sometimes parents physically abuse their children. It's not easy to tell on a parent. Almost all parents love their children, and children love their parents. But sometimes a parent doesn't know the abuse is wrong. Some parents think it's okay to spank very hard, or to hit children very hard with an object. Other parents might hurt their children when they have problems they are worried about. Parents who abuse might also be angry at other people. But that doesn't mean it's okay to hurt their children.

- There are many people who can help abused children. Robin told the social worker at school about being hurt by her mom. Later, she visited the doctor, and the doctor called Child Protection Services. Child Protection Services is a group of people who work to keep children safe from abuse. They also help parents learn that abuse is wrong and that they should not hurt children. Child Protection Services are in every state in the United States.

    Police also work to keep children safe from abuse. Sometimes, children are hurt very badly. The police may be called to take the children out of the home. This is not done to punish the children. It is done to keep them safe while their parents get help.

- Parents and other adults who abuse children need help so they can stop hurting children. When they are sorry and tell the truth like Robin's mother, they can get help. They might see a social worker and talk over their problems. They might meet with a group of adults and talk about their problems. This is what treatment is. During treatment, the adults go to meetings. They learn how to be angry without hurting their children. This might take a long time.

When adults lie and say they did not hurt children, or when they hurt very, very badly, they might have to go to jail or to a special hospital to get better. But, most adults who abuse children and who get treatment stop hurting children.

So remember, children have the right to be safe. Adults do not have the right to abuse children. If you are getting hurt, you should tell so the hurting will stop.

Places to Get Help

A child who is being physically abused needs to tell about it. Here are some people and groups who can help.

Places to get help:

The family: Your parents
Your aunt, uncle, or cousin
Grown-up brothers and sisters
A grandmother or grandfather

At school: A teacher
A social worker
A school nurse
A friend

In the city or town: A police officer
A neighbor
Someone from Child
Protection Services
A doctor or nurse

Words to Know

absent (AB·sent)—missing from a place

abuse (uh·BYOOZ)—to hurt someone or to do wrong

accident (AK·sih·dent)—something that happens when you didn't know it would happen

behave (bee·HAYV)—to do what a person is supposed to do, like following rules

bruise (BROOZ)—a colored mark on a person's skin caused by being hit by a person or thing

Child Protection Service (CHYLD proh·TEK·shun SER·vis)—a group of people whose jobs are to protect children from all types of abuse

clinic (KLIN·ik)—a place where sick or

hurt people see a doctor in his or her office, but do not stay overnight

discipline (DIS·uh·plin)—training people to follow the rules

examine (egs·AM·in)—to look at carefully

foster home (FAWS·ter HOHM)—a home where children live with adults like a family, but where the adults are not their real parents

misbehave (mis·bee·HAYV)—do something a person is not supposed to do, or break rules

physical abuse (FIZ·ih·kuhl uh·BYOOS)—when an adult hurts a child and it's not an accident

problem (PROB·lem)—something that causes trouble and worry

serious (SIHR·ee·us)—when something is important and perhaps dangerous

social worker (SOH·shul WORK·er)—a person whose job is to help people with their problems

stitches (STIHTCH·uhs)—a kind of sewing with needle and thread. Doctors use stitches to close up bad cuts a person gets

stress (STRES)—problems that are not easy to solve and that cause someone to worry

treatment (TREET·ment)—special help that is given to people who have sick bodies or who need to learn new ways to act to stop abusing others

welt (WELT)—when a place on the skin swells from being hit

Note to Adults

In a survey of 150 first, third, and fifth graders, we found that 47 percent of the children could define physical abuse. When asked which types of discipline were okay for parents to use, they favored the following: sending to their rooms, grounding (restricting to home or yard without friends), no television, yelling, and withholding allowance. Surprisingly, 65 percent said spanking was okay and 22 percent said hitting with a belt or stick was okay. When asked about this, children said a little hitting was all right, but "when the hitting turns into a beat-up" it becomes child abuse.

It has been estimated that each year 125,000 new cases of physical abuse occur in the United States. Physical signs of abuse are bruises, welts, burns, fractures, lacerations or abrasions, abdominal injuries, and central nervous system injuries. Behavioral signs of abuse to a child may be defiance, unhappiness, negativism, anger, destructive difficulty with relationships, or excessive need for attention.

If you suspect physical abuse of a child, ask the child if he or she will tell you what happened to cause the injury you noticed. Many children are afraid to report parents or have been told not to, as Robin was. They don't know that being injured or hurt by a caretaker or parent is against the law. Young children like their parents and think that whatever discipline measures they use are acceptable.

If a Child Reports Abuse. . .

When a child reports abuse, a report must be made to Child Protection or the police. They will decide what should be done to protect the child.

- Reassure the child that he or she did the right thing in reporting the abuse. Add that you will help the child be safe.

- Explain to the child that the Child Protection worker or police will help the child be safe. They will also help the parent get treatment to learn how not to abuse.

- Occasionally, a case of abuse will not be handled properly and the child will continue to be abused. This is very damaging to the child's trust in adults. It is very important to tell the child that, if he or she is still getting hurt later, he or she can come tell you again and you will help.

About the Authors

Deborah Anderson, Executive Vice President of Responses, Inc., has helped establish programs to aid both children and adults whose lives have been touched by abuse and neglect. Deborah developed and directed a sexual assault services program for the Hennepin County (Minnesota) Attorney's Office, and created the conceptual basis for Illusion Theater's internationally acclaimed production, "Touch," which presents information on abuse to children. Deborah has worked with students, teachers, and school administrators regarding child abuse and neglect, and has been nationally recognized for her work in the area of children as victims or witnesses in court.

Martha Finne, Director of the Children's Division of Responses, Inc., joined that organization after directing a survey of Minneapolis school children entitled, "Child Abuse and Neglect: From the Perspectives of the Child," the basis for these books. She has worked as a child abuse consultant, speaking to parent groups and elementary school staffs regarding child abuse and its prevention. Her background includes a degree in social psychology, counseling at the Bridge for Runaway Youth, and volunteer experience working with both public schools and social service agencies.

About Responses, Inc.

Responses to End Abuse of Children, Inc. is a public nonprofit corporation which tries to coordinate programs in all segments of the community aimed at reducing family violence and child abuse and neglect. The organization works with both the private and public sectors to develop the most constructive responses to these problems.

In 1983 and 1984 Responses, Inc. conducted a survey of Minneapolis school children to assess the children's knowledge on various aspects of child abuse and neglect. The responses to the survey provided the framework for these Child Abuse books.